MARKUS MOTUM

DUCKS OVERBOARD!

WALKER BOOKS

AND SUBSIDIARIES

LONDON • BOSTON • SYDNEY • AUCKLAND

Hello.

You may have seen rubber ducks like me before, but none of them has a story like mine. I've been on quite an adventure. This is the story of my incredible journey — where I came from, how I got lost, the peculiar sights I saw, and how I ended up here.

Where is here?
Well, first things first.

My story began
in 1992 in a
factory in
China.

The factory moulded
plastic bath toys in the
shape of ducks, frogs,
turtles and beavers.

Many toys are made from plastic because it is safe,
long-lasting and easy to clean.

Thousands of us ducks were packed up together ...

Plastic can be an extremely useful material and is used widely in medicine, technology and food storage.

ready to be put in big containers and sent across the world, destined for a bathtub somewhere.

More plastic has been produced since 2004 than during the whole of the twentieth century.

Our container was loaded onto a ship with hundreds of others destined for Washington State, America – about 6,000 miles across the Pacific Ocean.

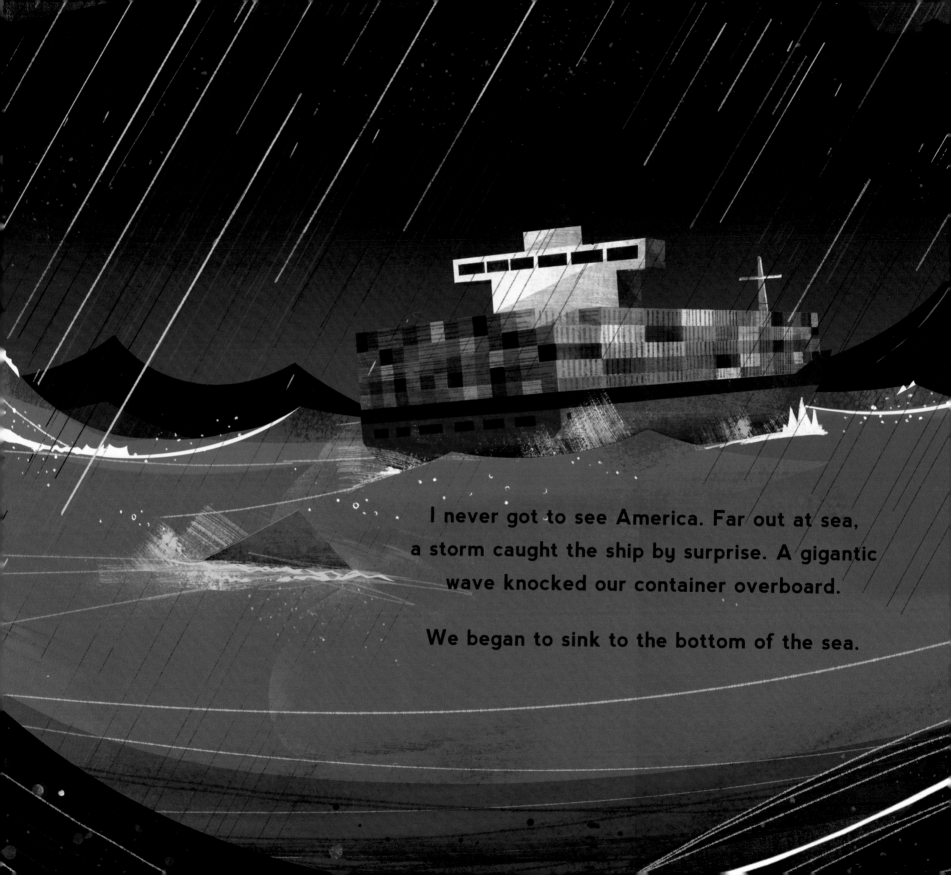

I never got to see America. Far out at sea,
a storm caught the ship by surprise. A gigantic
wave knocked our container overboard.

We began to sink to the bottom of the sea.

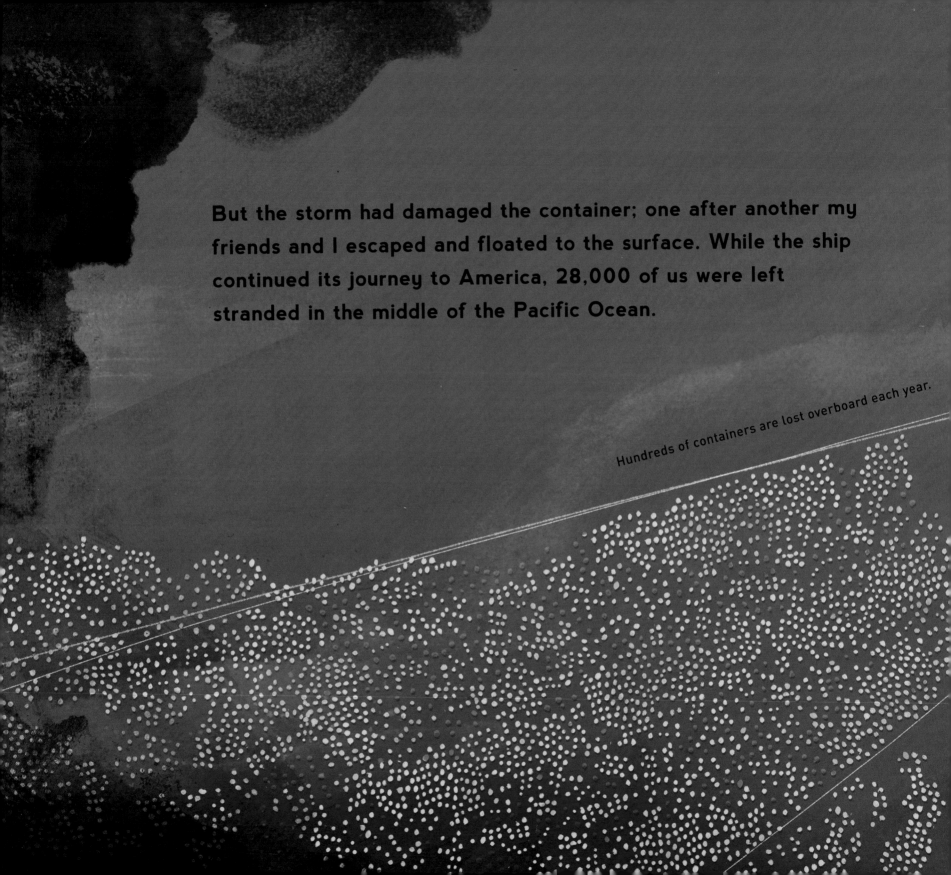

But the storm had damaged the container; one after another my friends and I escaped and floated to the surface. While the ship continued its journey to America, 28,000 of us were left stranded in the middle of the Pacific Ocean.

Hundreds of containers are lost overboard each year.

Cargo found floating or washed up by the sea is known as flotsam. Most flotsam is never recovered.

We were buffeted and blown by the wind and the waves, and were soon spread out across the water. Ocean currents pulled us in different directions.

Currents are what move the water in our oceans around the world. They are driven by wind and tides.

We were surrounded everywhere by the blue ocean and the life in it.

We saw fish of every shape and colour and enormous jelly fish.
Then we spotted something that was far stranger ...

a plastic bag.

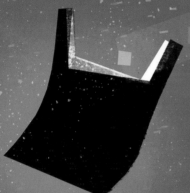

Plastic bags are "single-use" plastic, which means they are used for a very short time before being thrown away.

Before we knew it, a passing
whale had gobbled it up.

Some sea creatures mistake plastic bags for food but it clogs their digestive systems.

The giant creature still looked hungry as it swam off to catch up with its pod.

As the days passed, we carried on our journey.

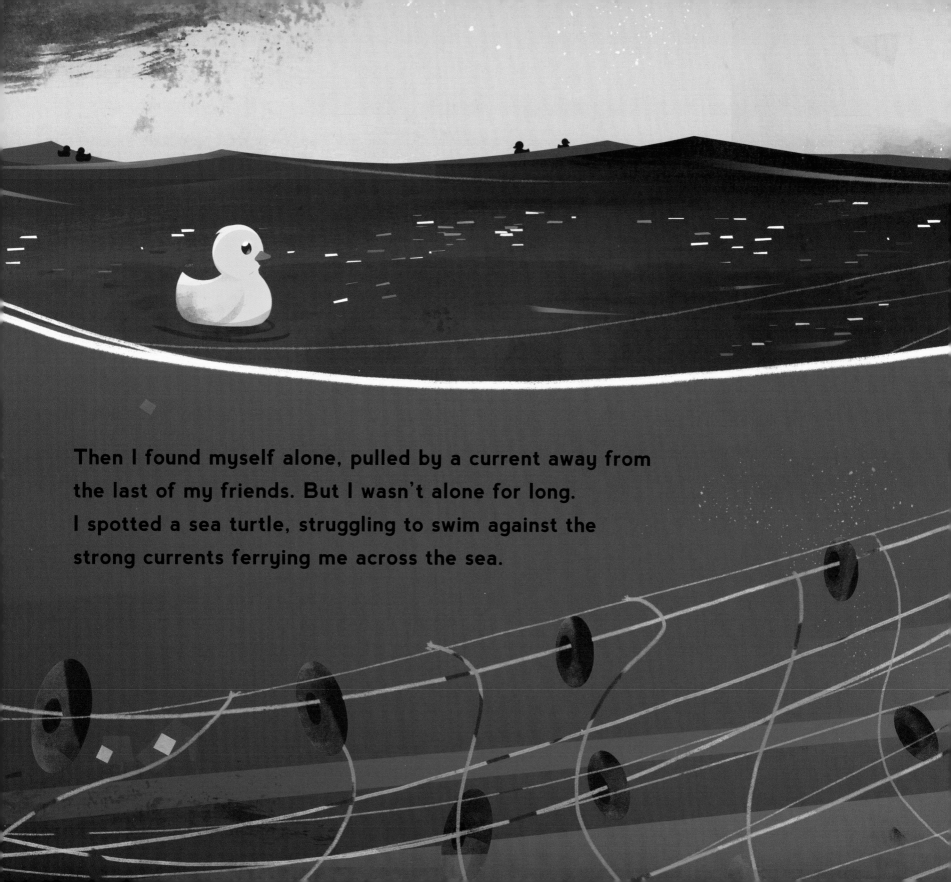

Then I found myself alone, pulled by a current away from
the last of my friends. But I wasn't alone for long.
I spotted a sea turtle, struggling to swim against the
strong currents ferrying me across the sea.

Plastic fishing nets dumped in the ocean can entangle sea creatures, preventing them from breathing, swimming or catching food.

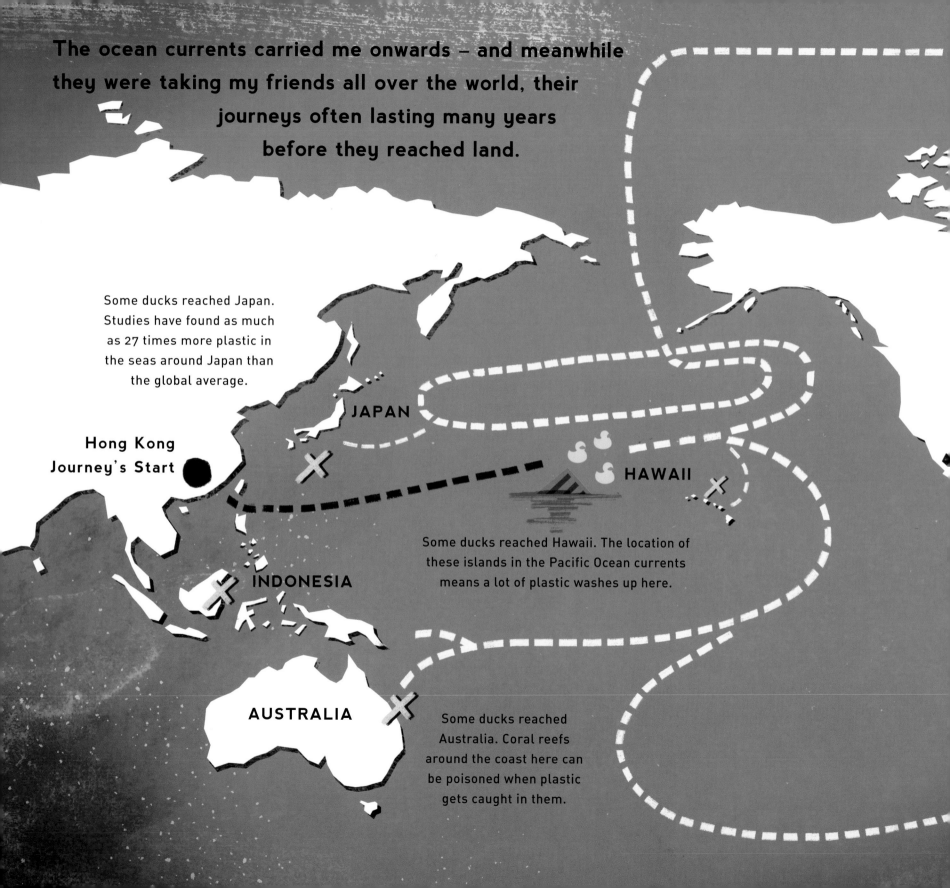

The ocean currents carried me onwards – and meanwhile they were taking my friends all over the world, their journeys often lasting many years before they reached land.

Some ducks reached Japan. Studies have found as much as 27 times more plastic in the seas around Japan than the global average.

JAPAN

Hong Kong
Journey's Start

HAWAII

Some ducks reached Hawaii. The location of these islands in the Pacific Ocean currents means a lot of plastic washes up here.

INDONESIA

AUSTRALIA

Some ducks reached Australia. Coral reefs around the coast here can be poisoned when plastic gets caught in them.

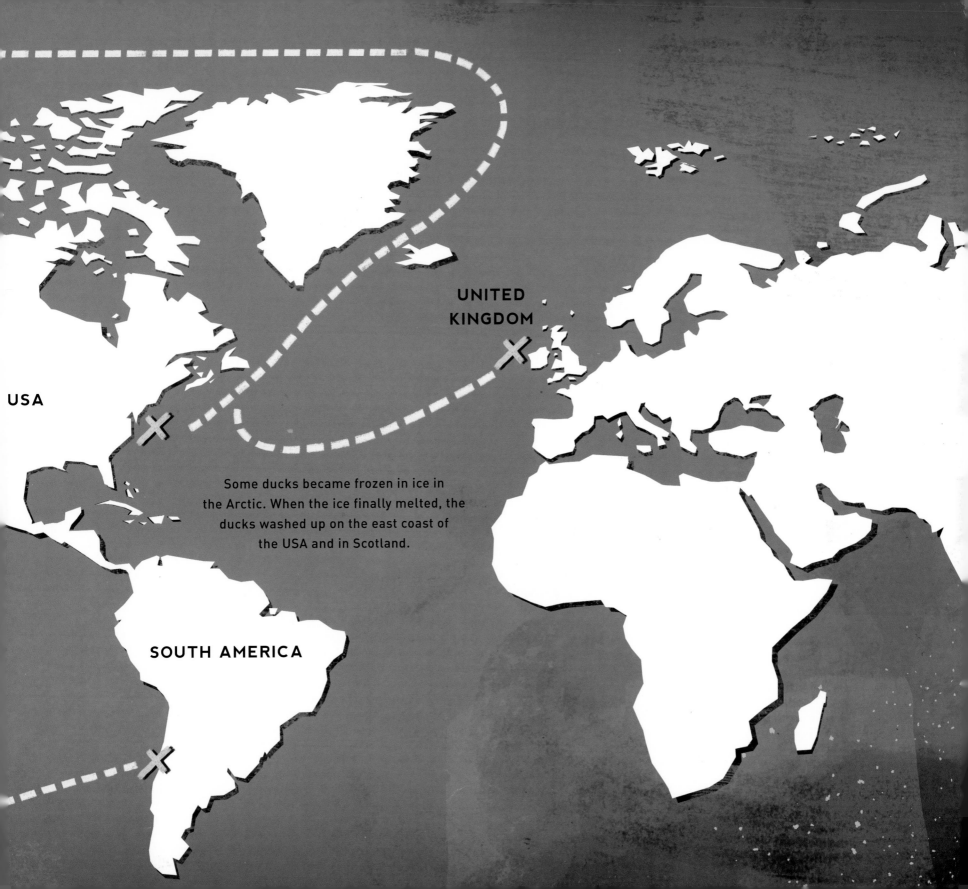

USA

UNITED
KINGDOM

SOUTH AMERICA

Some ducks became frozen in ice in
the Arctic. When the ice finally melted, the
ducks washed up on the east coast of
the USA and in Scotland.

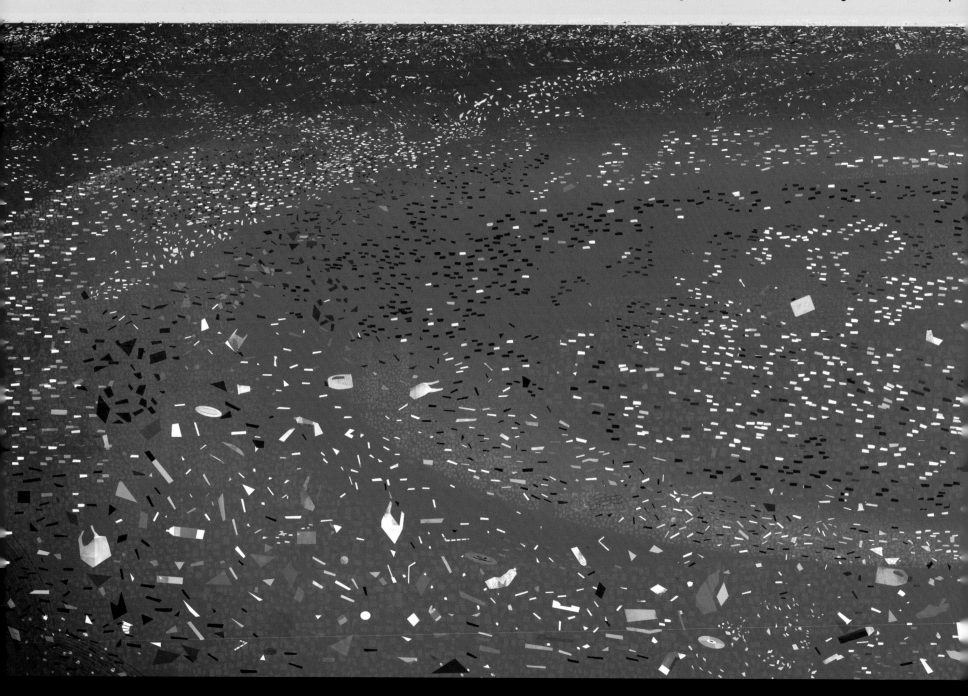

I wasn't so lucky. The wind and currents took me into a rubbish patch.
For miles all I could see were toothbrushes, bottles, cups, shoes and more.

It is created by swirling currents that carry debris here and trap it. It is estimated to be more than double the size of Texas.

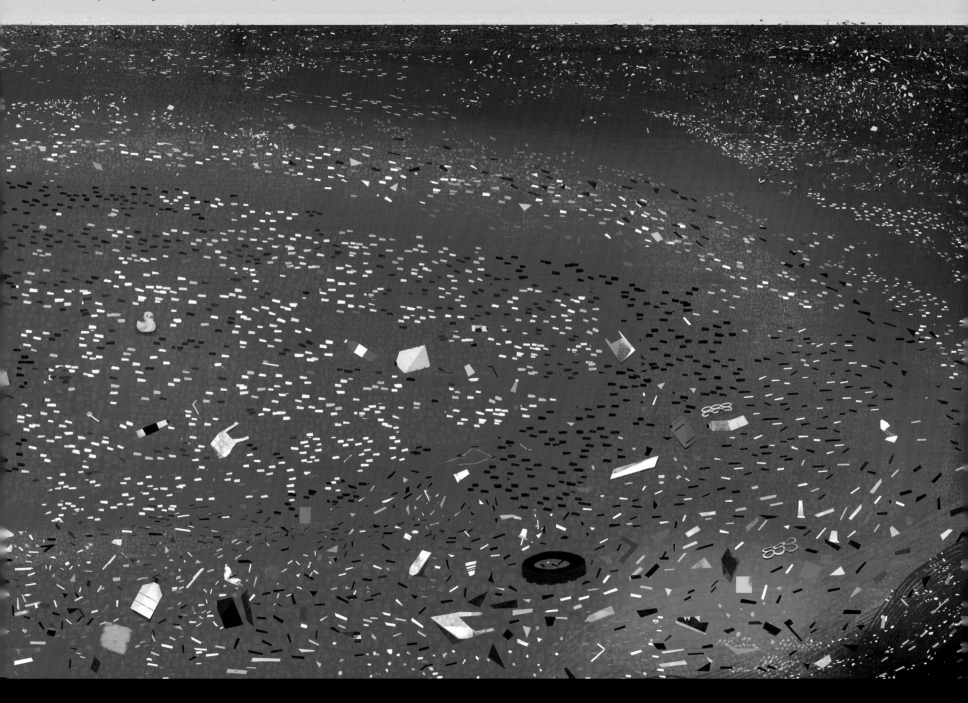

I had found a giant swirling area of forgotten rubbish. Did I belong here?

I thought I'd be stuck as unwanted rubbish for ever. This was the rubbish the humans had forgotten. No one seemed to care.

But eventually the winds grew stronger and the waves grew larger. Giant clouds blackened the sky above me as a storm broke out.

Over weeks,

months and years,

the ocean waves
tossed me back
and forth.

I floated for thousands of miles, until one day I finally spotted land. I had never seen this place before, yet I recognized something very familiar.

I washed up onto a shore to discover it was covered in rubbish, just like everything I thought I had escaped.

But here the rubbish was not being forgotten or ignored. All across the beach, the debris was being collected and organized in order to be recycled, so that these unwanted items could be useful once again.

As I watched the plastic on the beach disappear, I wondered where I would end up.

And it was here!

LOST AT SEA

Hundreds of shipping containers are lost at sea each year. The container that spilled into the Pacific Ocean in January 1992 was filled with plastic ducks, frogs, turtles and beavers. Scientists such as Curtis Ebbesmeyer tracked the journeys of these toys, asking beachcombers to report any they found washed up on shore. The routes of this "flotsam" revealed the worldwide network of ocean currents.

Most of the plastic toys from that container have since been found all over the world, but it's believed about 2,000 are still at large, possibly trapped by currents or even ice. Who knows where they will eventually land?

OCEAN CURRENTS

The water in our oceans is constantly on the move. We call these movements ocean currents. Winds, tides and the rotation of the Earth affect the direction and speed of currents. Currents move heat, sea creatures and flotsam (including plastic ducks) around the oceans.

A gyre is where rotating currents create a massive whirlpool. Where floating plastic meets a gyre, it creates patches of rubbish, the plastic moving round and round in a big soup. There are at least five giant "garbage patches", in the North Atlantic, South Atlantic, North Pacific, South Pacific and Indian Ocean. There may be more.

PLASTIC FACTS

✳ Much plastic can be reused or recycled. However, 40% of plastic produced is single-use, which can stay in the environment for hundreds of years after being used for only a few minutes.

✳ It is estimated that 8 million tonnes of plastic rubbish enters our oceans every year.

✳ Plastic never disappears. It only breaks down into smaller and smaller pieces – known as microplastics – until you can't see it. These microplastics are harmful to sea creatures that eat them.

✳ By 2050, it is predicted that there will be more plastic (by mass) than fish in the ocean.

HOW YOU CAN HELP

✳ A beach clean is a great way to stop plastic and other rubbish getting into our oceans. You can find out more about how to take part from the 2 Minute Foundation at beachclean.net. Who knows, you might even find a lost yellow duck!

✳ If you don't live near the sea, there are still ways you can help keep plastic out of the ocean. Always recycle what you can, and put your rubbish in bins – this helps keep plastic out of rivers, which lead to the ocean.

✳ There are lots of projects that have been launched to tackle our plastic problem, some of which you can get involved in. Kids Against Plastic was launched by teenagers Amy and Ella Meek, and campaigns to reduce "single-use" plastics. Find out more at www.kidsagainstplastic.co.uk. The Ocean Clean Up was started by eighteen-year-old Boyan Slat in the Netherlands to develop technologies to get plastic out of our oceans. Find out more at theoceancleanup.com.

✳ You can also make your voice heard by signing petitions against single-use plastic or contacting your local MP.

For Isabella and Adriana

First published 2021 by Walker Books Ltd, 87 Vauxhall Walk, London SE11 5HJ

2 4 6 8 10 9 7 5 3 1

© 2021 Markus Motum

The right of Markus Motum to be identified as author and illustrator of this work has been
asserted by him in accordance with the Copyright, Designs and Patents Act 1988

This book has been typeset in Nevis

Printed in China

British Library Cataloguing in Publication Data: a catalogue record for this book is available from the British Library

ISBN 978-1-4063-9311-8

www.walker.co.uk